GREAT AFRICAN-AMERICAN ATHLETES

TAYLOR OUGHTON

DOVER PUBLICATIONS, INC.

Mineola, New York

PUBLISHER'S NOTE

The 46 African-American athletes represented in this book were chosen mainly for their athletic accomplishments which, by all accounts, are extraordinary. However, in addition to their excellence as competitors they are also people who have overcome the obstacles facing them with determination and self-confidence, achieving what they did as much by hard work and dedication as by natural talent. They are not only representative of the accomplishments of the African-American community in athletic competition, but examples of dedication and sportsmanship for everyone to aspire to.

Bibliographical Note

Great African-American Athletes is a new work, first published by Dover Publications, Inc., in 1996. The publisher gratefully thanks Cheryl Wagner at the Basketball Hall of Fame and Peter Fierle at the Pro Football Hall of Fame for their assistance.

International Standard Book Number: 0-486-29319-X

Manufactured in the United States of America
Dover Publications, Inc., 31 East 2nd Street, Mineola, N.Y. 11501

HANK (Henry) AARON (1934–   ) was born in Mobile, Alabama. He grew up playing baseball in sandlots, using a stuffed sock as a ball. After playing for the Negro National League, he was signed by the Milwaukee (now Atlanta) Braves. Within four years he led the League in home runs and helped the Braves beat the Yankees for the world championship in 1957. His home-run count rose steadily until, in Cincinnati in 1974, he tied Babe Ruth's record of 714 home runs and, four days later, passed it. By the time he finished his career, Hank Aaron's home-run total was 755, making him the greatest home-run hitter in baseball and securing his place in the Baseball Hall of Fame.

KAREEM ABDUL-JABBAR (Lew Alcindor; 1947–) was recognized as a star while still in high school. In his first year of college at UCLA, he led the team to an NCAA championship. That was in 1966, and UCLA did not lose a single game until Kareem was injured during the season two years later. At 7′2″ and 225 pounds, Kareem Abdul-Jabbar was incredibly agile and managed to outwit and outmaneuver his opponents at every turn. Playing for the Milwaukee Bucks, he was among league leaders in points for three consecutive years (1969–72), was named the NBA's Most Valuable Player six times and, by the end of his career, which he finished in Los Angeles, he had broken Wilt Chamberlain's all-time scoring record with 38,387 points.

MUHAMMAD ALI (1942–   ) began his career as Cassius Clay, winning the light-heavyweight gold medal at the 1960 Rome Olympics. After the games, Clay turned pro and, in 1964, defeated Sonny Liston for the world heavyweight title. That same year he changed his name to Muhammad Ali (he had already become a Black Muslim). In the late 1960s, Ali was stripped of the title and banned from boxing for refusing to serve in Vietnam, and it wasn't until a court decision in 1970 that he was allowed to return to the sport. Ali, with his war cry, "I *am* the Greatest!" staged a remarkable comeback, beating George Foreman and regaining the heavyweight title in 1974. Defeated by Leon Spinks in 1978, he won the title a record third time before retiring in 1979 as one of the greatest and most recognized fighters in the world. His definitive retirement was in 1981.

"Hurricane HANK" (Henry) ARMSTRONG (1912–1988) began his professional career in 1932 and by 1938 held the feather, light and welterweight titles. Armstrong remains the only boxer ever to hold the title in three different weight classes simultane- ously. Although he lost the featherweight and lightweight belts after only one year, he remained welterweight champ until 1940 with 20 successful title defenses. Hank Armstrong retired in 1945 and was inducted into the Boxing Hall of Fame in 1954.

ARTHUR ASHE (1943–1993). Born in a poor neighborhood in Richmond, Virginia, Arthur Ashe began playing tennis at the age of seven. He was soon recognized for his skill, intelligence and determination and, in 1963, became the first African-American man named to the Davis Cup team. NCAA championships in men's singles and doubles led to his first major title, the U.S. open men's singles championship, in 1968. Widely respected for his calm, intelligent style of play, Ashe continued to move up in the ranks of men's tennis, finally winning the men's singles title at Wimbledon, the most prestigious title in tennis, in 1975. Forced to retire from competition because of heart problems, Ashe continued to promote athletics in a number of youth programs and charities which he remained involved in until his death from AIDS in 1993. He is considered one of the great competitors and great sportsmen of the twentieth century.

Louisiana-born sprinter EVELYN ASHFORD (1957–   ) competed in four Olympics from 1976 to 1992. An All-American sprinter and one of the first women to receive an athletic scholarship to UCLA, she qualified for the U.S. Olympic team in 1976 but was not able to compete because of the 1980 American boycott of the games. Setting a world record of 10.79 seconds at the 1981 World Cup, Evelyn Ashford went on to compete in the 1984 Olympic Games in Los Angeles. There she won gold medals in the 100m dash, tying her world record and setting a new Olympic record, and in the 4 × 100m relay. In the 1988 Olympics in Seoul, she won a silver in the 100m dash and a gold medal in the 4 × 100m relay. At age 35, in the 1992 Barcelona Olympic Games, Evelyn Ashford won her fourth gold medal as part of the 4 × 100m relay team, making her the oldest American woman to earn a track-and-field medal in the Olympics.

JAMES "Cool Papa" BELL (1903–1991) spent his career in the Negro National League. Bell led the Homestead Grays to three consecutive World Series (1943–45) and played in nine All-Star Games. Cool Papa was one of the fastest runners to play in the Negro Leagues, so fast that he could make it from first to third base on a bunt. A master of the inside-the-park home run, Bell batted .417 his rookie year (1922) and finished his career with a lifetime average of .337—better than that of Willie Mays and Hank Aaron! Bell was inducted into the Baseball Hall of Fame in 1974.

VALERIE BRISCO-HOOKS (1960–), a short sprinter in high school and at California State, Northridge, set her sights on an Olympic gold medal early. In 1984, Brisco-Hooks made the U.S. Olympic Team and traveled to Los Angeles to compete in the Summer Games. While there, she won gold medals in the 200m dash, the 400m run and the 4 × 400m relay, setting Olympic records in each event—the first American woman to win three gold medals in Olympic track-and-field competition since Wilma Rudolph. The fourth fastest performer of all time in the 400m run, Valerie Brisco-Hooks also appeared in the 1988 Olympic Games in Seoul, winning a silver medal in the 4 × 400m relay.

JIM BROWN (1936–   ) played for the Cleveland Browns from 1957 to 1965 and is still considered to be the greatest runner in football history. An All-American out of Syracuse and the Browns' number-one draft pick, he was named Rookie of the Year and went on to play in nine consecutive Pro Bowls. During his nine years with the Browns, he led the NFL in rushing 8 times, was named All-NFL each of those eight years, and was the League MVP twice. He set the all-time rushing record of 12,312 yards, which stood for 22 years and, although Walter Payton finally broke his record, it took Payton 13 seasons to do what Jim Brown had done in nine. Brown was inducted into the Football Hall of Fame in 1971.

ROY CAMPANELLA (1921–1993) made his Major League debut in 1948 with the Brooklyn Dodgers. As a catcher for the Dodgers, Roy Campanella was voted the National League's MVP three times and, in 1953, set single-season records for home runs (41), RBIs (142) and putouts (807) by a catcher. His career was cut short by a car accident in 1958 that left him paralyzed.

WILT CHAMBERLAIN (1936–   ), another two-time All-American, at 7′ 1″, was called "The Stilt." He left college to play for the Harlem Globe Trotters and, after one season with them, signed with the Philadelphia (now Golden State) Warriors. He immediately drew the spotlight when he became the first, and only, professional basketball player to score 100 points in a single game. Once he was traded to the Los Angeles Lakers, Chamberlain became enormously famous, being named to the All-Star Team seven times and voted MVP in his last championship game in 1972. Wilt Chamberlain was the NBA's high scorer for seven years running, averaging 50.4 points per game in one season. By the time he retired, he had over 30,000 career points and held the all-time scoring record.

LARRY DOBY (1924–   ) was the first African-American to play in the American League. Signed by the Cleveland Indians in 1947, several months after Jackie Robinson began his career in the National League, Doby led the Indians to the World Series in his second season, and his heavy hitting (his series average was .318) helped them win it. In 1954 Doby again cleared the way for the Indians to win the Pennant by leading the American League with 32 home runs and 126 RBIs. After playing for the Chicago White Sox and the Detroit Tigers, Larry Doby retired from active playing in 1959 but continued to coach until 1978.

JULIUS "Dr. J" ERVING (1950–   ) attracted the attention of the Pros while playing at the University of Massachusetts before being snatched up by the Virginia Squires. With a dazzling offensive style, Dr. J led the New York Nets to two ABA championships in 1974 and 1976 and was the League's top scorer for three years running (1973–76). Traded to the NBA's Philadelphia 76ers, Dr. J continued to perform, leading them to the NBA championship in 1983 and being named the League MVP in 1981.

GEORGE FOREMAN (1949–   ) was a champion heavyweight, winning the heavyweight gold medal at the Mexico City Olympic Games in 1968. Five years later, as a professional, he beat "Smokin' " Joe Frazier to win the world heavyweight title. With his crushing right and a reputation for being impossible to knock out (up to that point, no one had ever even knocked him *down*), Foreman seemed unbeatable. Then he met Muhammad Ali. In 1974, in the eight-round fight billed as the "Rumble in the Jungle," George Foreman was knocked out for the first time. After his loss Foreman left boxing, vowing never to return. In 1987, however, Foreman came out of retirement and in 1993, at the age of 45, he again won the heavyweight title by beating Michael Moorer, making George Foreman the oldest heavyweight champion in the history of boxing.

Zina Garrison (1963–   ). The 1988 Olympic Games in Seoul marked the first Olympic tennis competition in 64 years and Zina Garrison, with her partner Pam Shriver, won the gold medal in women's doubles competition. Garrison also went on to take the bronze in women's singles and, after the games in Seoul, continued playing on the professional circuit. She won the 1988 mixed doubles championship at Wimbledon. Zina Garrison won a second Wimbledon mixed doubles championship in 1990.

ALTHEA GIBSON (1927–   ), the daughter of a South Carolina sharecropper, moved to Harlem while still a child and began playing tennis. By the age of fifteen, she was winning tournaments as a member of the American Tennis Association and, in 1956, won her first major title: the French women's singles championship. Over the next two years (1957–58) Gibson won the American national singles title twice, the women's singles title at Wimbledon and was ranked number one in the United States. By 1960, she was the top-ranked player in the world—the first African-American woman to achieve that status. In 1963 Gibson left tennis and joined the professional golfers' circuit. She was inducted into the National Lawn Tennis Hall of Fame in 1972.

JOSH GIBSON (1911–1947) never received the recognition he deserved, playing for the Homestead Grays of the Negro National League in the 1930s and 40s. He is considered the best heavy hitter to play in the Negro Leagues, reported to have hit eighty home runs in a single season, and is the only man ever to hit a ball out of Yankee Stadium. According to some, Josh Gibson wasn't just the best hitter in the Negro National League, but the best hitter ever to play the game. Gibson was voted into the Baseball Hall of Fame in 1972.

Attending college at California State University, Northridge, FLORENCE GRIFFITH-JOYNER (1959–) won the NCAA championship in the 400m run and placed second in the 200m dash in 1983, and won a silver medal in the 200m dash at the 1984 Olympic Games in Los Angeles. In her second Olympic appearance, at the 1988 Summer Games in Seoul, Griffith-Joyner, nicknamed "FloJo," came into her own. She won gold medals in the 100m dash (setting an Olympic record of 10.54 seconds; she had set the world record earlier that same year), the 200m dash and the 4 × 100m relay, and a silver medal in the 4 × 400m relay. FloJo had emerged as the world's fastest woman and America's most celebrated track-and-field athlete. When she retired in 1989, *Runner's World* said she "could be fairly called the 'greatest sprinter of all time.'"

REGGIE JACKSON (1946–   ) got his start with the Kansas City Athletics in 1967 and moved with them to Oakland the next year. Reggie made a name for himself as a heavy hitter, leading the American League in home runs four times, and was voted League MVP in 1973. Playing for the Yankees in the 1977 World Series, Jackson hit five home runs, breaking the record Babe Ruth had set in 1926 and leading the Yankees to a world championship.

A running back out of Auburn, "Bo" (Vincent Edwards) JACKSON (1962–   ) was an All-American and Heisman trophy winner in 1985. He went on to play for the Los Angeles Raiders beginning in 1987, was named Outstanding Rookie, and was selected for the 1990 Pro Bowl. In addition to his career as a professional football player, Bo Jackson played in the Major Leagues as an outfielder for the Kansas City Royals, the Chicago White Sox and the California Angels. In 1989 Jackson was one of the American League's top home-run hitters with 32 balls out of the park and 105 RBIs, and played in the All-Star Game. His career was plagued with injuries that finally forced him to retire from professional sports altogether in 1995.

"MAGIC" (Earvin) JOHNSON (1959–   ), with his spectacular passing skills, has made team basketball an exciting and glamorous thing to watch. In twelve seasons, he led the Los Angeles Lakers to five NBA championships, won three League MVP awards and three Finals MVP awards, was named to nine All-NBA First Team selections and played in 12 All-Star Games. One of Johnson's greatest challenges, however, came in 1992 when he discovered he was infected with the HIV virus. He announced his retirement from the NBA but played on the gold-medal-winning U.S. Olympic Basketball team at the 1992 Olympic Games in Barcelona. After leaving basketball, Magic spent two years using his celebrity to teach AIDS awareness and raise money for research, receiving the NBA's J. Walter Kennedy Citizenship Award for his tireless efforts. In 1996 Magic Johnson made another stunning announcement—he was coming out of retirement, a decision he rescinded at the end of the season.

JACK JOHNSON (1878–1946), after running away from home at the age of 12, met Joe "The Barbados Demon" Walcott, one of the great early welterweight champs. Johnson learned enough sparring with Walcott to convince himself he could make a living as a boxer. He rose slowly through the heavyweight ranks, finally winning the title from Tommy Burns in 1908 and becoming the first African-American heavyweight champion. Jack Johnson, with his cautious style and a knack for provoking the crowd, was one of the least-liked champions in boxing. He held the title for seven years, finally losing it to Jess Willard, who defeated Johnson in a 26-round bout in Havana, Cuba, in 1915.

RAFER JOHNSON (1935–) attended UCLA and did not compete in his first decathlon until his senior year. He was so successful at the ten-event competition that he continued to train for it and won a spot on the 1956 Olympic Team. At the Olympic Games in Melbourne, he put on a spectacular performance and won a silver medal. Determined to be the best in the world, he set new decathlon records in discus, pole-vault, javelin and the 400m run in 1958. At the 1960 Olympic Games in Rome, his determination paid off with a gold medal as he easily defeated the competition and set a new decathlon record of 8,392 points, shattering all previous records.

MICHAEL "AIR" JORDAN (1963–), now one of the most recognized sports figures in the world, began his professional career with the Chicago Bulls and was named Rookie of the Year in 1985. Nicknamed "Air" Jordan for his incredible hang time, the 6'6" guard set a playoff record in his second season with 63 points in one game against the Boston Celtics. It was the beginning of an all-out assault on the record books. Leading the NBA in scoring with an average of 30 or more points per game for seven consecutive seasons (tying Wilt Chamberlain's record), Jordan was named League MVP four times, part of the NBA All-First Team eight times, and made ten All-Star Game appearances. As a leader, he guided the Bulls to three consecutive NBA championships and was part of the gold-medal-winning Olympic Basketball team in 1984 and 1992. In 1993, Jordan unexpectedly announced his retirement from basketball to play Minor League Baseball in the Chicago White Sox system. His retirement was short-lived, however; with a baseball strike during the 1994–95 season, Jordan returned to the Chicago Bulls, whom he led to a fourth championship in 1996.

JACKIE JOYNER-KERSEE (1962–   ), considered by *Ebony* to be the best female athlete in the world, is known primarily for the heptathlon. The heptathlon is a multievent competition consisting of the 100m hurdles, high jump, long jump, shot put, 100m dash, 200m dash and 800m run. It is divided into two days of competition and is considered the most grueling of the track-and-field competitions. In 1984, Joyner-Kersee won the silver medal in the Olympic Games at Los Angeles, and in 1988 won the gold at the Olympics in Seoul, setting a world record of 7,291 points. At Seoul she also set Olympic records in the 100m dash and long jump, and a world record in the 200m dash. In addition to her gold medal in the heptathlon, Jackie Joyner-Kersee also won a gold medal in the individual long jump competition—the first woman to win a gold medal in both a multievent competition and an individual event in 64 years.

RICHARD "Night Train" LANE (1928–) was signed as a defensive back by the Los Angeles (now St. Louis) Rams in 1952, after four years in the Army. A deadly open-field tackler, fast, agile and aggressive, "Night Train" Lane loved to take gambles on the field and was known for making spectacular plays. During his rookie year with the Rams, Lane set a new single-season interception record with 14 passes picked off. He played for the Chicago (now Phoenix) Cardinals and the Detroit Lions during his thirteen-year career. "Night Train" retired in 1965 as the record holder for career interceptions with 68 for 1,207 yards and five touchdowns, was named All-NFL five years, played in six Pro Bowls and was voted All Time NFL cornerback. Richard "Night Train" Lane was inducted into the Hall of Fame in 1974.

WILLIE LANIER ("Contact"; 1945–) was the Kansas City Chiefs' number-two draft pick out of Morgan State. Linebacker Lanier used his speed and quick thinking to become the anchor of Kansas City's powerful defense. Nicknamed "Contact" for his ferocious tackling, Willie Lanier was the defensive star of Super Bowl IV, where the Chiefs upset the Minnesota Vikings for the championship. During his ten-year career, Lanier was named All-AFL/AFC seven times, played in two AFL All-Star Games and six Pro Bowls, and missed only one game in ten seasons. Willie Lanier retired in 1977 and was inducted into the Football Hall of Fame in 1986.

"SUGAR" RAY LEONARD (1956–) was named after the legendary singer, Ray Charles, and added "Sugar" to his name, after the great middleweight boxer Sugar Ray Robinson. He dreamed of winning an Olympic gold medal but didn't want to make a lifelong career of boxing so, when he won the welterweight gold medal in the 1976 Montreal Olympics, he announced, "My dream is fulfilled," and refused to turn professional. However, financial pressures and a simple love for the sport forced him back into the ring within a few years. With his trademark grin and blurring speed, Sugar Ray quickly made it to the top, winning the WBC welterweight title in 1979, the WBA junior-middleweight belt in 1981, the middleweight title in 1987, the light-heavyweight title in 1988, and the super-middleweight title later that year. He retired in 1989.

At a high school awards ceremony, CARL LEWIS (1961–   ) met the legendary track star Jesse Owens. Owens' advice to Lewis was: "Dedication will bring its rewards." Encouraged by his parents, Carl Lewis followed this advice, training and competing with self-confidence and dedication, and made it to the 1984 Olympics in Los Angeles. There he achieved his goal, winning gold medals in the 100m dash, 200m dash (setting an Olympic record of 19.8 seconds), long jump and the 4 × 100m relay (with a world-record 37.83 second time)—the first winner of four gold medals in a single Olympics since Jesse Owens. In the 1988 Olympic Games in Seoul, Lewis also won gold medals in the 100m dash and long jump, and a silver in the 200m dash. In the 1992 Olympics in Barcelona, Lewis won gold medals in the 4 × 100m relay and the long jump. In 1996, in Atlanta, he won a gold medal in the long jump. Named Athlete of the Year by *Track and Field News* in 1982, '83, and '84, Carl Lewis is one of the all-time great athletes in the history of track and field.

JOE LOUIS ("The Brown Bomber"; Joseph Louis Barron; 1914–1981) was born on an Alabama cotton plantation. He was to become the second African-American heavyweight champ. Nicknamed the "Brown Bomber" for his relentless combination punching, Louis won the title in 1937 when he defeated James J. Braddock in Chicago. Louis went on to defend the title 25 times and retired as a champion in 1949. Unlike Jack Johnson, Joe Louis was one of the best-loved heavyweight champs for both his incredible skill in the ring and his quiet dignity outside of it.

Beginning with his unprecedented move from high school directly to professional basketball in 1974, MOSES MALONE (1955–) became one of the game's all-time centers. In the NBA's all-time top ten for points, rebounds, field goals, free throws and number of games, he was ranked third for career points (27,360) and first for consecutive games (1,207) at the end of the 1994–95 season. Playing for the Houston Rockets, then for the Philadelphia 76ers, alongside the legendary Dr. J, Malone was League MVP three times, Finals MVP in 1983, a six-time rebounding champion, and helped power his teams to two NBA championships. After 12 All-Star Games, and 20 seasons in the NBA and ABA, Malone played his 45,000th minute during the 1994–95 season and was the last player left in the NBA who also played in the ABA.

WILLIE MAYS (1931–   ) signed with the New York (now San Francisco) Giants in 1951. He was drafted into the Army after his rookie season, but returned in 1954 to lead the Giants to Pennant and World Series wins, hit 41 home runs and be named Most Valuable Player. Nicknamed the ''Say Hey Kid,'' he astounded fans, leading the league in stolen bases four times, hitting three triples in one game in 1961 and again being named League MVP in 1965. He was elected to the Living All Time Baseball Team in 1971 and, when he retired in 1973, Mays was the third all-time home-run hitter, behind Hank Aaron and Babe Ruth, with 660 balls out of the park.

CHERYL MILLER (1964–   ) is the most recognized player in women's basketball. Tremendously athletic and graceful, Miller made it an airborne sport. From 1982 until 1986 she was the star forward of the USC basketball team. The first player ever to be named All-American four years in a row, Cheryl Miller led the Trojans to NCAA titles in 1983 and 1984, was named Naismith Player of the Year three times, Tournament MVP twice, and became the second all-time scorer in women's basketball with 3,018 career points. In international competition, she led the United States Olympic Basketball Team to a gold medal in the 1984 Olympic Games in Los Angeles. Named the best male or female player in college basketball by *Sports Illustrated* in 1986 (her senior year), she became the first USC athlete to have her jersey retired when she graduated. Cheryl Miller was inducted into the Basketball Hall of Fame in 1995.

EDWIN MOSES (1958–   ) dominated the 400m hurdles for over a decade. In his first Olympics, the 1976 Games in Montreal, Moses won the gold medal for the 400m hurdles by eight meters and a world-record time of 47.64 seconds. It was the largest margin of victory in that event in Olympic history. Following his gold medal in Montreal, Moses began an incredible series of victories, not losing a race for ten years. During that time, he broke his own world record twice, in 1980 and again at the 1984 Olympic Games in Los Angeles, won his second gold medal and was named Athlete of the Year by *Sports Illustrated*. His 107-race winning streak finally ended in 1987, but he still qualified for the 1988 Olympic Games in Seoul and earned a bronze medal there. Edwin Moses was inducted into the Track and Field Hall of Fame in 1994.

ISAAC MURPHY (1861–1896) won his first horse race in 1875, when he was only 14 years old. In a sport where, since colonial days, nameless black jockeys (often slaves before the Civil War) rode while the wealthy owners of the horses bet on the outcome, Isaac Murphy was so skilled that his name became known during his lifetime and he remains one of a handful of jockeys whose fame is legendary in the sport. He compiled an incredible string of victories during his career, including three Kentucky Derbies (two consecutively) and four of the first five American Derbies. No one has ever repeated Isaac Murphy's three Kentucky Derby wins or matched his lifetime record.

JESSE OWENS (1913–1980) was born in Danville, Alabama. Throughout his high-school and college career, he was recognized as a track phenomenon. At Ohio State University, in 1935, he set three world records *in one day*. His greatest moment, however, was in the 1936 Olympic Games in Berlin. Adolf Hitler and the Nazi party were in power in Germany at that time, and they boasted that their athletes' performance in the games would prove their theory of Nordic racial superiority. Owens set Olympic records in the broad jump and 200m dash, tied the world record in the 100m dash, and ran on the 400 × 100m relay team that broke both the Olympic and world records. Jesse Owens won four gold medals, defeated Hitler's "Supermen," and was voted the greatest track-and-field star ever by the Association of Sportswriters.

ALAN PAGE (1945–   ) was an All-American defensive tackle out of Notre Dame and the first-round draft pick of the Vikings in 1967. With extreme strength and speed, and quick reflexes, Page was named NFC Defensive Player of the Year four times. During his nine years with the Vikings and three with the Chicago Bears, Page played in 236 consecutive games, including four Super Bowls, was named All-NFC/AFC nine times and played in nine Pro Bowls. He retired in 1981 with 173 career sacks, 23 fumble recoveries and 28 blocked kicks. Alan Page was inducted into the Football Hall of Fame in 1988.

"SATCHEL" (Leroy Robert) PAIGE (1906–1982) is considered one of the greatest pitchers in the history of baseball. Playing in the Negro National League, Satchel Paige once pitched five winning games in one week and, in his 31–4 season with Pittsburgh, had 21 consecutive wins. He took the Kansas City Monarchs to a Negro League championship in 1942 with 64 straight scoreless innings. Paige was finally admitted to the Majors at the age of 43, where he pitched his first game for the Cleveland Indians—a shutout. He retired in 1953, but not before being chosen as the pitcher for the 1954 American League All-Star Team.

WALTER PAYTON (1954–   ) was a first-round draft pick out of Jackson State University in 1975. As a running back for the Chicago Bears, Payton quickly established himself as a superstar. At 5'10" and 202 pounds, he was small for the position but made up for it with speed and surprising power. During his 12-year career, Walter Payton had 77 games over 100 yards and set the single-game rushing record of 275 yards. He was named All-Pro seven times, played in nine Pro Bowls and remains the all-time rushing leader, having broken Jim Brown's record with 16,726 yards and 110 touchdowns. Walter Payton was inducted into the Football Hall of Fame in 1993.

OSCAR ROBERTSON ("The Big O"; 1938–   ), is considered by some to be basketball's greatest all-around player. Robertson was signed by the Cincinnati Royals in 1961 after he led the U.S. Olympic Basketball Team to a gold medal at the 1960 Olympic Games in Rome. While in Cincinnati, Robertson helped his team to six straight playoff appearances before being traded to the Milwaukee Bucks. There the Big O, along with Kareem Abdul-Jabbar, led the team to the NBA championship in 1971. Robertson played on the All-Star Team every year of his career and held the all-time record for assists with 9,887 when he retired.

JACKIE ROBINSON (1919–1972) was spotted playing for the Kansas City Monarchs of the Negro National League in 1945. Branch Rickey, head of the Brooklyn Dodgers, was so impressed that he signed Robinson immediately, making him the first African-American to play in the Major Leagues. He was 1947's Rookie of the Year and, two years later, led the League in stolen bases and was voted the National League's MVP. Jackie Robinson is best remembered for breaking down the color barrier in baseball and clearing the way for the integration of all professional sports.

"SUGAR RAY" ROBINSON (Walker Smith; 1920–1989) enjoyed a long career, during which he first won the world welterweight title in 1946, holding it for five years before moving up to middleweight. After beating Jake LaMotta ("Raging Bull") in a bout for the middleweight belt, Robinson held the title five separate times between 1951 and 1958—a record not likely to be broken. Considered the greatest and one of the most colorful middleweight champions in history, Sugar Ray Robinson fought an unbelievable 202 bouts during his 25 years in the ring.

WILMA RUDOLPH (1940–   ) overcame crippling childhood polio to become an Olympic sprinter. She competed in the 1960 Olympic Games in Rome, winning the 100m dash, the 200m dash (setting an Olympic record of 23.3 seconds in that event) and ran the anchor leg for the United States' 400m relay team, which also won a gold medal. Wilma Rudolph, considered the fastest woman in the world, was the first American woman to win three gold medals in Olympic competition and, not surprisingly, was voted Female Athlete of the Year by both the Associated Press and the European Sportswriters Association.

BILL RUSSELL (1934–) revolutionized professional basketball with his approach to defense and shot-blocking. A two-time All-American, Russell was the star of the 1956 U.S. Olympic Basketball Team and helped win a gold medal at the Games in Melbourne. As a pro, his duels on the court with Wilt Chamberlain were legendary. Bill Russell led the Boston Celtics to eight consecutive championships (11 total), was named MVP five times and was a starter on the All-Pro Team three times. In 1966, he became the coach of the Boston Celtics—the first African-American to coach a professional basketball team.

GALE SAYERS (1943–   ), an All-American halfback out of Kansas, was feared by NFL defenses for his exceptional breakaway speed. During his 1965 rookie season with the Chicago Bears, Sayers scored a first-season record of 22 touchdowns and never looked back. The next year he was the leading rusher in the NFL. By the end of his career in 1971, Sayers was the NFL's lifetime leader in kickoff returns, had been named the Pro Bowl MVP three times, All-NFL five times and, in 1969, was voted the All Time NFL halfback. He was inducted into the Football Hall of Fame in 1977.

HERSCHEL WALKER (1962–) became a national sensation while still at Georgia Tech. As a running back, Walker was a three-time All-American, named College Football Player of the Year in 1982 and won the Heisman Trophy that same year. He began his professional career in the now defunct USFL with the New Jersey Generals and, in 1985, was named USFL Player of the Year. Walker was signed by the Dallas Cowboys in 1986, played in the Pro Bowl in 1986 and led the League in rushing with 1,514 yards in 1988. He was traded to the Minnesota Vikings in 1989 and then, in 1992, to the Philadelphia Eagles where he became the only NFL player to have a run from scrimmage, a pass reception and a kickoff return of 90 yards or more in a single season. He played the 1995 season for the New York Giants and now plays for Dallas again.